The Dice Throwers

Poems by Douglas Cole

Liquid Light Press

Premium Chapbook First Edition

Copyright © 2015 by Douglas Cole

ISBN-10: 0990926745

ISBN-13: 978-0-9909267-4-0

Liquid Light Press

poetry that speaks to the heart

www.liquidlightpress.com

The cover art is *The Soldiers Casting Lots for Christ's Garments*, a drawing by William Blake (©The Fitzwilliam Museum, Cambridge) Cover design by M. D. Friedman (*www.mdfriedman.com*) Photo of poet by Jennifer Merritt

Contents

In The Beginning

Heaven is far from the things of earth,
but it sets them in motion by means of the wind.
- I Ching

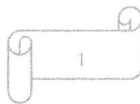

The Father

My father dreams the red spider dream
in his lonely hotel room far from home.
The phone is ringing but he won't answer it,
knowing it will only open to the drunken
flood of his wife's voice complaining
about the sewer and her migraines,
the renters who won't pay,
a new glitch in the treadmill.
He looks out on a city, somewhere
(he can't remember which one),
at the cranes, the stock yards,
the industrial river and perpetual night.
Another drink, another lidded streetlight
comes on like the sloppy women in the lounge,
with their jet talk and smiles,
to him another part of all the meetings,
the deals and the precious contracts
he mules across the time zones.
When at last he sleeps that final sleep,
the rooms around him alive
with the fury of the end of the world
parties and the television drone,
he throws the universe into silence
absolute, everything now eclipsed
like a flame snuffed out by a fist.

The Curiosity Shop

I went into the shop
where the mermaid hung
with its bared teeth and hollow eyes,
and I saw the stillborn faun,
the sea-horse and the shrunken heads,
and Sylvester in a glass case standing,
my sister behind me chanting,
Sylvester, Sylvester, the man who got shot!
He stood with feet above the ground,
his flesh taught and shining,
his eyes narrowly dreaming.
And I looked hard beneath his hand
for the circle of the bullet hole,
there beneath his wrist,
his arms crossed over his chest
as though he were trying to hide it.
And then I heard him speak to me,
saying through his desiccated lips:

Take me back to the desert.
I'm naked in this case,
reliving the day I fell
not knowing or even seeing
the one who shot me
and left me alone to die.
For three days I lingered
with a bullet in my spine,
unable to rise, flesh burning

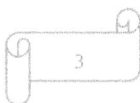

as I begged the sky for death.
Then vultures dropped down
and plucked out my eyes.
These you see are only glass.
Strangers found me and hauled me off
to became a freak attraction
in roadside carnival tent shows,
children marveling at my corpse,
and I've stood a hundred years
stone still and silent, waiting
for these bones to disintegrate.
So, I think, take me back there
where something went wrong
and maybe I'll be released.

Then he was still once more
beneath the monkey corpse
and the glazed swordfish,
there with his cryptic mate,
Sylvia, a woman who froze
to death in the mountains and lay
with her flesh gnawed by rats
so that the fibers of her lungs
show through the bare spaces,
and like him she was brought
down and hung here on display,
hunched with indelicate open jaw.
And year after year I returned
to listen at his glass,
but he never spoke again.

The Black Road

If I were to direct a film of hell
    I would set it in Aberdeen

    close up of the junky
   sitting on the bank of the river
below the bridge where
  the water turns grey
    widening by the lumber stacks
  under green banners of timber support
    and the resistant turned away

  logging mill gorged and erupting
     white smoke that rides above
   the taverns and the motels
     Wishkah ghosts wandering North
away from the claw of Gray's Harbor

  Aberdeen roads coiled in the blood
and the lumber moving South
  where we always face
    every man for himself
     with rules for himself
  in a long bad dream
    lingering in the homes below
     the Hoquiam Mansion

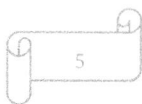

The Swing

Smoke from a passing truck curls
over the hedgerow as I watch
the girl in perpetual motion
swing back and forth beneath
the elm tree behind her house.
With the shades always drawn
and wind ticking in the screens,
I wonder what she sees
inside, nightly, an only child
with parents who won't allow
her to return my wave, who
shuttle her in the back of a van
and keep her bound by invisible hands
wrapped around their corner lot.

I imagine inside her home
a mother and father with advantages
but no luck, looking on with fault-
finding eyes gone cold by a grinding
sense of the shortage of money,
the living room a grim echo
of their unspoken thoughts,
a mantle clock scything away,
rows of mysterious ancestors stone
still in photographs on the walls.
Her room is perfect, and she checks
her chores on a weekly list.

She will not speak unless bid to.
Never have I seen a friend come over,
never has she gone to the nearby field.

She climbs instead upon her swing,
nudged into movement by the wind,
riding with her legs stretched
out in the surge of her body's power,
hands gripped into the braids of rope,
some urge drawing her higher
and higher as her face turns to sky.
She pushes from her tethered arc
up through the arms of the elm,
and the neighbor's dog runs after her,
the whisper of a house falling back
as she ascends through pale leaves
in waves of individual flames.

And I see her free above the city,
beyond all luck in a wild current,
riding a storm that rips the clouds
and plunges all homes into darkness.
Nightly she rises, parents wandering,
calling through the trees but never
looking up to see her high overhead,
turning in a lathe of stars.

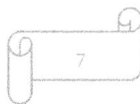

Crossing Guard

He walks out
      toothless and grim
into a river of traffic.
      His black coat blacker
in the rain,
      his glasses two white discs,
he might as well be
      invisible.
But with his only shield
      a flimsy rubber sign
with the word "stop" written on it,
      he could as easily block
a river as these drivers
      who halt
when he raises his arm,
      the prophet's fire
flashing in his eye.

Birth

Behold the sun exploding over high grass,
this field, these arms raised
to that opening from which I've come.

Alligators prowl the shadows.
I will sing you a song of the blue man
and woes that have come and gone.

This is what the willow knows.
A dog leaps out of the glare,
running in the pure fury burning

elemental in his limbs. I know
that fire, the crows stunned into flight,
the black wings expanding into light.

And I go out, sent out with a compass
and a coin for the toll, my only
orders to come back by darkness.

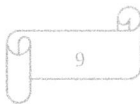

The Open Ward

Come away, O human child!
To the waters and the wild
With a faery, hand in hand,
For the world's more full of weeping than you can understand.

                - W.B. Yeats

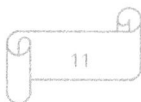

Arch Street

Childhood ended between the Siskiyous
and Yreka as my mother, sister and I
drove south in our old Volkswagen
loaded with all our crap falling off
along the freeway. We lost things
I can't even remember as we moved
in perpetual reduction of space
through Berkeley student housing
meagerly furnished with broken-down
beds and desks carved in by years
of migratory seminary students.

Friends I made were outlaw children,
and we broke into every building,
especially Benton Hall with its high
windows looking down and out on
the flatlands and the fiery bay
and the Transamerica Pyramid.
We absorbed *World At War*
and played our own games of war,
rock fights in construction sites
that always came to a brutal end
with curses and spoils of proud
scars we bore as noble decorations.

Exploding fluorescent lights became
the universal destruction in delight.
And we had our great epics, too,
like the story of John-John flying
through the plate glass window,
high and cut and crazy laughing,
bleeding all over as he lurched away.
And every day the sky went dark,
the schoolyard flooding with smoke
that rose from the city incinerator
as children screamed in unison
to the sound of the air-raid siren.

Through the maze of Cal Campus,
thieves denned in Eucalyptus groves,
darkness crowned Strawberry Creek
as I walked beneath the buzzing
street lamps up Seismograph Hill,
making my way by perfecting
the mask of invisibility or threat
to pass safely through the quadrangle
and the alleyways, as moonlight slid
like blood down our duplex door.

The Angel

The first time I saw
the angel coming down,
I didn't know what it was.

At first it seemed a speck,
then it seemed a mist.
I saw one bright crescent blade
cutting through the sky,
carving through the trees,
superscripting every home
down Shattuck Street to school.

And as it approached it grew
into a web of lighting,
weaving along the corridor walls
as if with some intent,
engulfing the rooms
and the children in their chairs.

Then it shot into my eyes,
opening, blinding me
with ecstatic limbs of light,
and as it flew back,
blazing through my mind,
I turned to follow
the lure of its bright
wings across a gulf of black.

West Campus

I hiked down Durant Street
each day of the bus strike, weaving through
the human flood of Telegraph Avenue
and the stench of back alley dumpsters,
climbing over the chain-link fence on my way
past the Permanent Transient Hotel.

I passed the chanting street philosophers,
with pigeons spraying from my feet,
and I crossed the confluence of Shattuck,
where faces leered from the halfway house
and inmates howled from their asylum.

I saw the dragon eating the world,
wind keening through abandoned homes
and rain twisting down the railroad tracks,
as I cut along the tilting backyard paths
under laundry lines of fluttering bed sheets,
with dogs snapping from their chains.

And every day the boy, Paris, appeared
out of nowhere, challenging me to fight him
for no reason at all. Until one day I found
a rusty horseshoe and beat him bloody to the ground
and left him on the tracks as I went on to school.

The Sickness

I remember a woman in Berkeley
who used to walk the hills cowled
in her scarf and dark glasses.
She kept her distance, spoke to no one,
but I learned how she became allergic
to the world, sensitized to chemicals:
her rugs, her sheets, her clothes,
as the walls of her home rejected her,
until the only room she inhabited
was the kitchen, alone. And she walked
the hills, alone, terrified of contact.

Andreus's father, a physicist, forgot
the names of his children, turned to stone
in the darkness of the living room,
lost in memory fragments, watching
his children become vague equations.
Then Andreus contracted stomach cancer,
living through chemotherapy pills
that he held every night in his hand,
knowing the nausea coming from each,
knowing their sickness in trade.

Eddie went mad and chained himself
to his girlfriend's car, plagued by Zeus,
combinations reeling through his mind,
deafening the world with bad intent.

The flower shop was a front for killers.
The democratic convention was full of spies,
the hills his haunt of endless wandering,
searching, talking wildly the dread nights
he fought the demons crackling in his head.

Something in a victim terrifies us,
and there, it seemed, disease ran rampant,
drove me through the Telegraph babble,
the carnival of hassles, the ruins of Cal,
furious dancers in the den of Sprowel Plaza
spinning their waves in the edgy night.
Now Old Man Valentine shuffles down
Arch Street to huddle by his stove for winter,
blue from the cold in a pin-striped suit,
and, smiling, hands me a leather key chain
that crumbles to dust in my hands.

San Francisco

buried me in the records department
of the UC Medical Center and cold fog afternoons,
reading *Naked Lunch*, smoking slow hours,
gave me a black eye the night I was drunk,
spinning, crashing into the coffee table,
knocked out, passed out, waking up
on Jimmy's floor with vision blurred,
like every morning on the Muni —
crickets set up camp in my head
with their coded Coit Tower chattering,
a gift of Eddie's nightmare, not mine —
mine was the party
(I can't remember the girl's name)
in that old house on Fulton, I think it was,
doing lines of coke in the kitchen,
and that skinny guy with some disease
(he still had the blue ink X's on his cheek
from radiation treatments)
passed me a straw he had just used,
and on the end of it I saw a drop of blood —
drunk, high, scared of disease,
I stumbled to the station that night,
waiting for the train, leg going like a piston
in that bright addled neon light,
thinking, could be me next,
as the ghosts unpeeled themselves
from the white tile walls.

Telegraph

The wasted washed out eyes
look right through you,
the afflicted, the lame, the lost,
the shades on parade,
glittering jewels on velvet stands,
smoky clusters in doorways,
the falafel spices, the cars, the horns,
the scammers, the beggars,
the wanting, weird boulevard of desires.
I earned my knowing by degrees.

Everything it taught,
I carry with me ——
the right gaze, the right walk,
the right maneuvers, the right guile,
the right glare, the right oblivion,
the right mantra, the right despair.

Remember Vacaville,
and Manson in his hole,
the Great America date with Suzanne Crough,
the Hilltop Mall, Albany, and Pinole,
KFOG, El Cerrito, and sad San Pablo.
I've driven here in so many vehicles,
cruised University Avenue
and West Campus, site of sorrows.
Where the liquor store used to be,

a Montessori school took hold.
Andronico's is faded but extant,
but La Tolteca is gone.

Nothing changes and everything,
shadows on the move
in a circus looking for a host.
I once plunged in with trepidation,
now I emerge with a wink and a grin —
greasy counters, disheveled souls,
children eating pizza on the curb.

Tales of Possession

If wishes were horses,
beggars would ride.
　　　　　　- An Old Saying

Ghost

One night an old woman appeared
at the door wanting answers,
directions to a social hall
long gone, asking about events
I couldn't remember or know.
Her hair was a wild cloud,
her coat a fragile covering
for a night just barely receding.
Bits of grass and dandelion seed
adorned her as if from this
she were made, and her eyes
were wild red-rimmed frantic
creatures of their own
in tireless search of something:
fields where houses now stood,
a perfect sky. And I was
a sad disappointment to her,
unable to provide one answer,
one bit of proof that the world
she sought for still existed.
Declining my offer to come inside,
to find someone who could help,
she waved her hand in a way
I knew meant I had disappeared.
And she wandered off
mute ranting, arm sweeping,
in a violent discourse of pure
energy sparking another dawn.

Search

I literally peel open
eyes from a void dream
and lunge back into
the bulk cage of a skull
with a stabbing hack
it's almost comical
but for the virus lingering
one red eye and a vague
fluctuation of fever
some nemesis sickness
that just won't leave me
and I creep through
the clammy hallway
into the sting of shower
and dress in the dark
drink gut grinder coffee
peering into the grey
world mist sliding
in this long dream
of faceless and anonymous
passengers at the bus stop
and all I can think of is
you out there somewhere
my will and desire
for you sweet angel
century after century
freak show after freak show
as I fly from dawn
to dawn sun to sun
looking for your light

Workers

The tired worker
        awakens in darkness.
His child's cries
        pluck him from
the far field of dreams.
        He hates his job at the warehouse,
and his wife hates
        his frustration.
Since the rains came
        a strange fever lingers
in his blood.
        The doctors don't understand.
He drives
        in the dark street,
green dashboard dials
        glowing on his child's face.
He loves the boy
        but fatigue makes
it hard to show,
        hard to rise
from his own bent form,
        as though his body
were trying to become
        a fist
to punch a hole in sky.

The Spot

There is a crazy woman
        who keeps hanging around the street corner.
She lives up the street in a dilapidated,
        as you'd expect, dark
window-shaded house with a yard
        grown up like a wild jungle,
somehow symbolic of her mind and
        most accurately resembling her hair.
She wears a filthy lambskin coat
        and hovers around the cross
that marks the spot
        where Beau Kirschner was killed
by a bus back in '95.
        It's like she's got a hold of something,
there, at this memorial of death,
        like she's guarding something
with her grim fierce eyes
        that rake everyone who goes by.
I'm not sure. I sometimes imagine
        she imagines it's her own child
who died here, and she's searching
        for his spirit. Or maybe she's got
hold of his soul and won't let it go.
        All I know is she attends
this spot like a vampire,
        as if the spot weren't haunting enough,
and makes of it
        a stranger vortex of energy,
as crows begin to circle
        and clouds slow to a halt above,
their shadows like a halo
        on her crouching form.

Permanent Transient

Bear up, my friend, this
darkness will not last forever.
Not even darkness can do that.
See, the light is immanent.
The buildings have begun
to glow like teeth.
I know your home like mine
is a transitory one:
hear the train passing below,
the traffic beginning above?
The ground trembles with motion.
And the worker bogmen are
rising from their beds.
But us, we are free.
Come and join our flock
gathering on Beacon Avenue.
Today there will be sun.
Today, we will ask that
sky dancer phantom who still
wears his costume of white
to take us with him
into his kingdom of air.

Knowing the Clue

Every day I search for clues.
        The trick is knowing
        the clue from the ruse.
An old man crossing guard
        nearly blind with black coat blacker
        from slick rain,
            holding a flimsy rubber "halt" sign
            and going out into the street
        in a neighborhood with no school
        no children present
            is a clue.
The crow looking down
        from the water tower is a ruse.
Light withdrawing
        from the face of sky
            is a clue,
        but the ensuing darkness is a ruse.
The Hammering Man statue
and the Lusty Lady peep show
            are certainly both clue and ruse,
            if you believe it.
Yet, a dream of flying from your body
        is neither clue nor ruse,
nor is the momentary arrest of the heart
        before awakening:
            these are simply the innocent
            motions of spirit rustling its cloak.

Know clues for their mystery

        and ability to reveal the divine;

        know ruses as tricks of the mind.

So, know when a word like "storm,"

        or the phrase, "I was in trouble once,"

        reach you out of a stranger's conversation,

            they are clues,

        but when the night whispers

            your name, it is only ruse.

A Messiah Who Never Comes

O dark dark dark. They all go into the dark...

-T.S. Eliot

Heber

Old Heber drank in the tavern
next to his produce store,
a warehouse of his own that
he bought with his wife's inheritance.
And he remembered how at first
he loved the work, how
purchase prices were low,
how he was making money
hand over fist, and thought,
could it get any better than this?

And the marriage was good,
though his step kids were sullen.
He thought in time that would change.
Then he and his wife had a daughter,
a beautiful child of his own,
and he went out onto the pier
and thanked God, lifting a glass
to toast the world as he gazed
upon the waters of the Sound,
celebrating life, higher and higher.
For a silent moment he breathed,
and everything became suspended
and clear as the Olympic peaks
on a day when the rains stopped.

But now it was dark,
and the rains returned,
and he was sick of the stench
of rotting leeks, the cold warehouse,

the rattle and crowds of the trolley,
every day going home to his wife's
slow growing coldness.
The step children hated him,
and he in turn hated their scrutiny.
He could never replace the first
father, his wife's secret wish
for the man whose photograph still
hung on the wall with judgment,
the one who had drowned
and was now perfect in death
and a constant shade in the house.

So Heber cast invisible lines
across the bar, trying to reel in
some overwhelming weight.
He took on a mistress who took
all his money, and day by day
his stories grew bleaker.
Did he always seek this,
even as it drew further away?

They finally dropped him
blind drunk in the yard,
still fighting his invisible fish.
And as he tried to rise and failed,
falling into the grey of dawn,
home spiraling madly before him,
his daughter appeared in the doorway,
little child in a bewildering doorway,
light falling from her open palms.

Marjorie

Before the maiden voyage,
she and her brother toured
the staterooms, the boiler room,
the galleys of the Titanic.
But on the day they were to sail,
their family missed it, simple as that.
So they crossed on the Carpathia
and picked up the survivors
where the great ship went down
with its freezing forms sinking
and small blue plumes rising
from depths distant and unreal.

In Michigan, her mother died,
poisoned by a miss-filled prescription,
and soon after that,
her father was struck dead by a car.
From grief, perhaps, or depression,
her aunt hanged herself
from a basement rafter.
All this true, all within five years.
And it had its effect on her mind,
as if life plucked from disaster
still had disaster to pay.

Her first husband, a strong
swimmer, drowned at La Push,
her second husband drank away
her money and abused her kids,
until she left him and on her own
worked night and day as a nurse,

barely able to be with her children
let alone show them love,
until they finally drifted on
and fast years flowed by
in which she lost her sight,
lost her hearing,
lost control of her hands,
as distant relatives came to say,
how wonderful to live so long
and reach such a rich old age.

How could they know
that some insane stranger on her street
arrived from time to time
and yelled at her, "You old bitch,
you old crow, die,
we hate you, die,"
even coming into her yard
and hitting her
so that later, though she had forgotten
in the haze of her aged mind
how it happened,
she found dry blood around her ear.

And no one knew
(how could they?)
what really drove her
day after day
to go out and sweep the dust
from her porch,
her sidewalk,
the street...
in the middle of that
blind and threatening wind.

The Passing

In the strange slow stillness
   of a loose circle they sit
     with nothing to say
  until the sudden announcement
    that the Grandfather has gone.

Silence unbroken, sunlight falls
  intermittently on the walls
    covered with family photographs,
  as the Grandmother asks the shades
    be drawn while abrupt words come,
rising to fill the vacant air.

Grandmother near and distant,
  "My drops," she says, "I need my drops."
And the soft relief falls upon
  her tongue in opiated riverrun
    blood to heart to hands and back.

The distant voice of the oldest son
  on the telephone arranging burial
    from the other room as the silent
  circle breaks with absurd and random
    topics: the capture of the arsonist,
     killers out of prison, prison costs,
taxes and capital punishment —

Grandfather drifts far above
  drinks and cigarettes in shaking hands
   and the lonely pull of love,
watching, watching alone
   outside them all, as he turns
    towards the opening white
   wings of a blazing sun.

The Journey

Where, whenas death shall all the world subdew
Our love shall live and later life renew.

- Spenser

To touch the core of the abyss

or to come so close you forget yourself,

to go so far and still be able to return,

to think yourself a saint with a saint's strength,

to die, to communicate this

annihilation sweeping through the blood,

through all the cells of senses overflowing,

and to rise again may be

the only true and beautiful art.

How many of those we know

who have gone

into the heart of darkness

have returned?

None unchanged, I'm afraid, ever.

For this I know: as one

holding the hand of the dying

sees the spirit gather over the forehead

curled like a question mark,

bewildered in the first moment of

deliverance,

going back into the hollow black

absence of the abandoned eyes,

the shadow of the doorway,

I cannot forget or even should

where we go
but return instead, turn again
with this knowledge
the living so strangely hunger for.

I cannot even say why I have gone
into the blind fury or
the still heart suspended
just beyond the pale mask,
the white wall, but
I have heard as you hear now
a voice across the gulf of time.

We cannot begin to explain wisely,
yet know if even fire consumes me,
and the anonymous void takes me,
my children and the great globe itself
back into the fist of space,
Energy, like a voice in the surging
chemical swarm of the brain,
will ignite another sun,
spit forth the sea's legacy far
more strange and real than all
we believe is real,
and I will find a stone skinned over
by the rivervein water,
and for a moment
which like a dream passes quickly,
I will remember you.

Elegy for Halvor

Ten more years will cover this grave,
the day of death already eaten away
to nothing more than a century.
Grandfather, this wind bears you
a perfect March storm circling the Sound
even as you turn from the sound of your
wife's voice begging, *Don't go, please don't go.*
How could you respond with a respirator
tube down your throat, your hands
useless as claws, unable even to write?
When your eyes gazed to the west,
I saw your spirit leap into a cloud.
Horses run with your memory.
I remember you in all storms,
a laughter you never had before,
cloaked inside your blue pipesmoke.
Medicine treated you wrong by wrong
diagnosis: a diabetic you never were.
And I remember that first real apple pie
you had after forty years of tasteless
Thanksgivings, ironic reward, prize too late.
How a factory ate away
the years you rode the Columbia,
the horse that was always in your blood
long after you lost the family claim
on a broken-down farm in Wenatchee.
No one could grow anything there.
I go back to it on roads that lead
finally away, signs that point in circles
as though to trick a stranger
and hide the ghosts that ride forever
to a farmhouse dissolving into hills.
And every time a storm comes in
and swings across the river,
horses rise up with flashing stars
that fly from their kicking feet.

The Journey II

I move through a narrow hallway
pipes overhead ticking
a nest of curling
steam snakeheads writhing
and come out into a courtyard
a gameboard of long-shadowed
marble figures

Here where the soul hesitates
one face in a window illuminate
and a siren somewhere far
back in the mind of night
I hear some movement
in the nearby trees
not wind but animal form
hovering in the black limbs
beyond the iron gate
hungry vultures circling
above the river bank

I follow
and stones roll underfoot
as hopeless wading in darkness
into the riverbed
current pulling
I let go
turn turn in a theater of water
music and voices
all around

The current has me
and I control only
my own small movement
more a question or a thought
a planarian twitching its own
unknown flesh
a few pulses registered
against a shell of cilia
and one feeble heart
pumping in a barely differentiated
pool of translucent blood
and still we call it living

The memory of the hotel
Paris and the blind man
the angel and the survivor
the magic coin
that brought me here
sickness unto death
the form in the trees
and I twist and arch
through the river blood
no notion of the shore
as I head now toward
the river mouth

Horses run against the sky
fire feathered from their spines
What form shall I take
among the gallery of faces
or should I dream
the mind of some phantom
some other vague inhabitant
at the border of vision

dropping from the sun
on nothing but the curve
my own wings design
on wind

With the siren coming closer
as I rise and fall
on the cool belly of the sea
my sea brothers calling
engine throbbing through
waves and ground and bones
approaching the lion
and the burning house
stars wheeling overhead
I realize the sound
like a surging wind cut down
through the narrow
tunnel of a fist is
my own voice
crying for birth

About the Author

Douglas Cole was born in Seattle, Washington, and grew up mostly in Berkeley, California, known then as 'The Open Ward.' After graduating from Berkeley High School, he attended college at the University of East Bay. After a year abroad, attending the University of Bradford in England and traveling throughout Europe, he returned to California to complete a Bachelor's degree in English at San Diego State University. Settling in Seattle, he taught English before finishing a Master's degree in Creative Writing at Western Washington University. He has worked as a clerk in the Brain Tumor Ward at The University of California Medical Center in San Francisco; construction in Los Angeles; catering in San Diego; house painting and teaching in Seattle.

Douglas Cole's writing has been published in *The Chicago Quarterly Review, Red Rock Review*, and *Midwest Quarterly*. He has more work available online in *The Adirondack Review, Salt River Review*, and *Avatar Review*, as well as recorded stories in *Bound Off* and *The Baltimore Review*. He has published two poetry collections, *Interstate*, with Night Ballet Press and *Western Dream*, with Finishing Line Press, as well as a novella called *Ghost*, with Blue Cubicle Press. He has received several awards, including the Leslie Hunt Memorial Prize in Poetry; the Best of Poetry Award from *Clapboard House*; and First Prize in the "Picture Worth 500 Words" from *Tattoo Highway*. He was also recently the featured poet in *Poetry Quarterly*. He is currently on the faculty at Seattle Central College and lives in Alki. His web site is *www.douglastcole.com*.

Acknowledgements and Credits

I would like to acknowledge the editors of the following publications in which these poems appeared:

"The Passing"	*Along the Path*
"Ghost"	*Connecticut River Review*
"Arch Street"	*Foliate Oak*
"Heber"	*Grey Sparrow Journal*
"The Spot"	*Isthmus*
"Birth"	*Jeopardy Magazine*
"West Campus"	*Jeopardy Magazine*
"The Father"	*Mankato Poetry Review*
"The Journey"	*Mandrake Poetry Review*
"Elegy for Halvor"	*Mandrake Poetry Review*
"The Journey II"	*Mandrake Poetry Review*
"Permanent Transient"	*Midwest Quarterly*
"Knowing the Clue"	*Penny Ante Feud*
"Marjorie"	*River Poets Journal*
"The Curiosity Shop"	*Ocean State Review*
"The Sickness"	*Spindrift*
"San Francisco"	*Underground Voices*
"Crossing Guard"	*Up the River*

Other Books from Liquid Light Press

All Liquid Light Press books are available directly from *liquidlightpress.com* or from any of the current major global distribution channels including Amazon, Barnes and Noble, the iBookstore and the Ingram Catalog.

Leaning Toward Whole by M. D. Friedman (Released June, 2011)
Explores the poignant and personal. Also available as a groundbreaking multimedia enhanced e-book.

The Miracle Already Happening – Everyday Life with Rumi by Rosemerry Wahtola Trommer (Released December, 2011)
A superb collection of poems is full of heart, humor, peace and wisdom.

Spiral by Lynda La Rocca (Released March, 2012)
A compelling poetic and melodic discourse from the persistent cravings and fears inside of each of us.

From the Ashes by Wayne A. Gilbert (Released June, 2012)
A true masterpiece that gnaws at the heart with universal appeal.

ah by Rachel Kellum (Released August, 2012)
This poetry has a simplicity and clarity that cuts to the core of being human.

Catalyst by Jeremy Martin (Released December, 2012)
Catalyst may just launch you on a fiery ride into yourself.

Of Eyes and Iris by Erika Moss Gordon (Released March, 2013)
Beautiful yet poignant in its simplicity.

Your House Is Floating by Susan Whitmore (Released June, 2013)
As smooth, crisp and satisfying as olive oil on fresh garden greens.

Nowhere Near Morning by Jeffrey M. Bernstein (Released October, 2013)
An intimate embrace of what it means to be alive.

Harmonica by Cecele Allen Kraus (Released March, 2014)
Harmonica bristles with a shimmering music that heals the heart.

Surf Sounds by Roger Higgins (Released October, 2014)
Expertly crafted and elegantly written, pulsing with the tides of the soul.

Black-Footed Country by Lindsay Wilson (Released March, 2015)
Like eating an artichoke, there are layers within thorny layers, each one more tender and subtle until finally you feast on the heart inside.

www.ingramcontent.com/pod-product-compliance
Lightning Source LLC
Chambersburg PA
CBHW021915040426
42447CB00007B/869